MOVING YOUR LIBRARY

Andrew McDonald

The Aslib Know How Series

Editor : Sylvia P. Webb

Routledge
Taylor & Francis Group

LONDON AND NEW YORK

 THE ASSOCIATION FOR INFORMATION MANAGEMENT

First published 1994 by Aslib
The Association for Information Management

Published 2015 by Routledge
2 Park Square, Milton Park, Abingdon, Oxon OX14 4RN
711 Third Avenue, New York, NY 10017, USA

Routledge is an imprint of the Taylor & Francis Group, an informa business

***

British Library Cataloguing in Publication Data
A catalogue record for this book is available from the British Library.

ISBN: 978-0-85142-328-9 (pbk)

Series Editor - Sylvia P. Webb

Sylvia Webb is a well known consultant, author and lecturer in the information management field. Her first book 'Creating an Information Service' was published by Aslib and has sold in over forty countries. She has experience of working in both the public and private sectors, ranging from public libraries to national and international organisations. She has also been a lecturer at Ashridge Management College, specialising in management and inter-personal skills. which led to her second book, 'Personal Development in Information Work', also published by Aslib. She has served on a number of government advisory bodies, is actively involved in professional education with Aslib and the Library Association and is also a former Vice-President of the Institute of Information Scientists.

Acknowledgements

Figures 3 to 7 are reproduced with the kind permission of both The British Library and Ernst & Young.

I should also like to acknowledge the assistance of Stephen Tanner, Director of Olympic Removals Ltd.

Contents

1. Introduction

Moving a library has been politely described as an 'unsettling experience'[1] and a 'chore'.[2] It has also, and perhaps more accurately, been referred to as an exhausting, frustrating, physical, dirty and essentially repetitive job. As Dr Johnson observed, "Change is not made without inconvenience, even from worse to better". Nevertheless, moving a modern library and information service is a substantial management challenge that is both logistically complicated and potentially stressful, and one which requires diverse qualities of leadership, vision and precision. Just when library staff energy has been depleted after a long building project, and will shortly be required to commission services in the new premises, it becomes diverted by the library move, an activity of which the library staff are unlikely to have had previous experience.

A well-planned move that is carried out successfully could be one of the most satisfying experiences that a librarian will ever have, but a poorly planned one can be catastrophic.[2] The key to success lies in careful forward planning, almost with military precision, with clear lines of responsibility and effective communication.[2,3,4,6]

The librarian has a crucial responsibility for the planning and management of the considerable amount of change involved in a move to ensure that library services are disrupted as little as possible and recommence quickly in the new premises. Disorder must be avoided at all costs since a mess may not be cleared up for many years and will detract from the quality of services offered. The librarian must take a lead role in organising staff, obtaining the necessary resources and influencing the other professionals involved to ensure a speedy and cost-effective move to the new site from which improved services can be provided in support of the parent organisation. The move is one small but significant part of the strategic development of the library service necessary to facilitate the delivery of better quality services from better planned space.

A successful move recognises the key importance of books, people and information technology in modern library and information services. Much of the modest literature published on library moves in the United Kingdom concentrates upon the procedural aspects and insufficient attention is paid to the crucial role of human resources in the process. Leadership, planning, control, teamwork and communication are all essential if the librarian is to achieve the 'vision' of improved services on the new site.

This book seeks to emphasise the principles and fundamental issues which must be considered in planning and implementing library moves. An over-prescriptive approach has been avoided since no two moves are alike.[3] In fact the variety of moves is bewildering. The new premises may be a new building, an extension or refurbished space. The library may be moving back into the same but remodelled space, or it may be moving within a building or into a different one several miles away or even in another country. The relocation may be part of a reorganisation or rationalisation within the parent organisation or company.[12,20] Moves where several libraries are merging present particular logistic challenges. Sometimes relocations are phased over a period of time for operational and economic reasons, and collections may need to be stored temporarily. In general, the published literature offers limited assistance because of the tremendous variety of the moves described, but there are underlying issues which the librarian must address whether moving a mobile library, a special library, a public library, an academic library, an archive, a special collection or an IT-based service. Nevertheless, planning must take account of the special problems and constraints relating to a particular library and its situation.

In common with other areas of library management, organising a library move involves coordinating a planned series of events and making decisions within a finite time scale and within the resources available. A successful move represents a substantial and visible achievement and will enhance the reputation of the library. Conversely, a disastrous one will inhibit the development of services and will leave its scars for many years to come.

2. Planning

The planning process

- Why is the move taking place?
- What are the objectives?
- What are the perceived benefits of the move?

All these are questions to which clear and positive answers are required.

When organising a move the library manager must not only be thoroughly conversant with the policy, objectives, layout, stock and services of the old library, but must also possess a clear 'vision' of how these elements can be integrated to provide better services in the new premises.

Space planning for the new premises is a complex discipline[2,6,15,26] discussion of which is outside the scope of this text but, clearly, the layout of the stock and the arrangement of services and staff must be planned in detail long before the move commences. Largely as a result of bitter experience, many librarians will endorse the importance of checking the floor loading of the new library. The area housing book stacks must exceed the minimum strength required (6.5 kN/m^2) but for maximum flexibility this level should be achieved throughout the building. Indeed, where mobile (compact) shelving is planned a floor loading of twice this level is a prerequisite. Several other factors influence space planning and these include :

- shape of the building
- fenestration
- building services
- size and nature of the stock
- equipment and IT-based services
- staffing levels
- staff and user work area requirements
- noise control
- security requirements.

The move may be part of an overall organisational move, or a crucial factor in the re-organisation of other departments or functions. Whatever the reason, it is inevitable and must be viewed as a unique opportunity to review service provision and the organisation of collections.[4,6] This should take account of the information audit and the results of an information needs analysis. Some libraries will have undertaken a fundamental reappraisal of their service objectives and this will have influenced the planning of the new facility. Others may simply wish to reorganise certain aspects of their collections, such as arranging periodicals alphabetically rather than in a classified sequence, or triggering the stock in preparation for an electronic book detection system, or bar-coding the stock for a new issue system. Whilst it may be attractive to make numbers of organisational changes as part of the move, the librarian should not be seduced into ambitious changes which, however desirable, will make the move more lengthy, complicated and frustrating than it might otherwise be. Most commentators advise completing changes in stock arrangement prior to the move and, where changes are proposed, the librarian must be convinced these are realistic and can be achieved. Clearly, it is advisable to discard or relegate all book stock and other items which are not required for the new site before the move. The importance of pre-planning is stressed by several contributors to a book edited by Mount.[35]

In keeping with current Japanese management theory, a move is generally characterised by a long planning period in preparation for a relatively short move. It is not uncommon for a two week move to have been planned for over a year. On the other hand, there has been a trend for shorter planning periods and removal contractors have recently been asked to quote for moves due to take place in a matter of weeks. Devotees of Total Quality Management will find library moves a fertile area for application of the technique. All concerned must be 'positively aligned' and committed to achieving the objective of relocating the library, and it is essential that all the procedures devised are 'right first time'.

Simplistically, everything to be moved should be identified, prepared for relocation and given a clear location in the new arrangement, and all the various elements organised within a coordinated sequence or timetable for the move as a whole. The move will be characterised by:

- the size and type of stock
- special items involved
- the location and nature of the old and new sites
- merging of collections and services
- the chosen method of moving
- the resources available, and
- organisational and service constraints.

The planning committee

Many libraries, especially larger ones, will set up a small planning committee especially for the move, typically composed of a move director and key circulation, building and administrative staff. Other members may include a representative of the organisation's Estates Department, Library Committee, the removals contractor involved and even a library user. The committee should have devolved responsibility and authority for all aspects of the relocation of the library - human resources and finance, as well as procedural and physical aspects. At an early stage they must recognise the critical constraints affecting the move in addition to the time and money available. For example, the move may be part of a larger company rationalisation, there may be institutional protocols to observe, and the size of library space available and the nature of the old and new sites will have considerable influence on planning.[5]

Library staff involvement and morale are crucial to the success of the move[2,4,6,7,10,14] and the committee must ensure effective communication with all levels of staff and provide the necessary training and information to ensure mutual trust and confidence. In particular, the committee must liaise regularly with the chief librarian, heads of department, library committee and also keep key organisation managers informed of progress. Whatever style of management is adopted in the library, the planning committee must provide the necessary leadership and direction for the move. Whilst it should communicate widely and encourage participation and teamwork in decision making, lengthy consultations and compromises may not be possible or desirable, and the committee must be capable of taking decisions and of communicating them clearly to all concerned.

A single project manager or move director is generally regarded as the best organisational approach - a known point of contact with full responsibility and authority for decision making and resources. The move director should be a senior member of staff (preferably at section head level or above) who is fully conversant with library policy and objectives, with plans for the new facility and with the arrangement of both the old and new sites. Above all the ability to be flexible and take decisions, often under stressful conditions, is paramount.

Timing

Clearly, the move must be timed to coordinate with the estimated completion and hand-over date of the new premises and after all the essential carpeting, shelving, furniture and equipment has been installed. Delays and complications are not unknown at this time even when all deliveries have been carefully planned so as not to conflict. Delays in completion rarely result from slowness in construction but most frequently arise because the time for supplying often large quantities of furniture is underestimated.[2] Most libraries will choose the quietest time of year (if there is one) to move when the inevitable restrictions in service will disadvantage the smallest number of users. An academic library will often choose the summer vacation. Public libraries may not enjoy such a quiet period. Some law, medical and special libraries are unable to close and may decide to move overnight or at weekends, or to move whilst trying to continue business as usual!

Many variables play a part in determining the length of the move including the amount and type of material, the number of helpers and the structural barriers to be overcome. Whilst librarians themselves can make estimates based upon sampling or indications in the literature, commercial movers are normally able to give much more accurate predictions and estimates. It should be remembered that experienced professional movers are likely to complete the move much more quickly than library staff or temporary helpers, especially where a large move of some distance is involved. It is customary to plan for completing the move in the shortest reasonable time, but quality and accuracy should never be compromised solely for speed.

Whilst it is extremely difficult to generalise about the time required to move books, a good removals contractor will normally be able to move 600-700 metres a day and, unlike untrained inexperienced personnel, will be able to sustain this level of activity. Much depends upon the nature of the building and the availability of lifts and the number of people involved in the move.

The geography of the building may be such as to permit a number of parallel moves with a consequent increase in speed. The book-moving rate predicted by one academic library was 1,120 linear feet per day for each crew and six crews could work in parallel with a proportionate increase in move-rate.[8] The British Library, despite certain physical constraints in its new building at St Pancras, estimate that 400 linear metres can be moved in a day.[9]

The length of time taken for various moves reported in the predominantly American literature vary greatly. One library managed to move 1 million volumes and its staff in fifteen days[10] whilst another moved only 600,000 volumes and 80 staff in five weeks. In a phased move it took an astonishing 155 days to relocate a 700,000 volume library.[11] Merging collections will normally take much longer - it took one academic library seven weeks to move 1½ million volumes and associated equipment from four buildings to one. The need to select and process books for moving will slow the rate of movement[12] - three weeks were required to move 10,000 titles selected from an academic library for relocation to an off-campus store.[13] Additional time will be required should the library choose to clean, repair, process or even fumigate books at the time of moving. Special collections require particular care and attention and hence rather longer periods for moving - 5000 cu. ft of rare books, records and manuscripts were moved in 5 days.[14] Moves will also take longer where the stock is housed in compact (mobile) shelving.

Publicity and public relations

Publicity is a crucial component in the success of a library move.[15] A good publicity campaign pays dividends because library staff and library users as well as staff in other departments clearly understand the purposes and benefits of the reorganisation. Well-prepared publicity brings about the understanding, confidence and support for library operations long after the project has been completed. Several librarians emphasise the value of good communication with users and management, especially where changed circumstances have necessitated alterations in the plans made for the move - 'libraries need friends'.[1,22] The organisation's management will in particular require reassurance on costs, timescale and slippages.[4] A gradual publicity campaign should be planned with each piece fitting into a whole programme. Some large libraries use the publicity expertise of move contractors or even public relations consultants. The library should exploit any suitable channel of communication to reach its staff and users but should always bear in mind that the purpose is to inform rather than discuss and communication should be regular and brief. Difficulty is frequently encountered in reaching non-users, remote users and those who are temporarily located away from the main organisation.

Internal publicity
Keeping library staff informed throughout the move process is essential and will facilitate the smooth operation of the project.[15] The library manager should not only utilise normal routes of communication, in which the value of e-mail cannot be overstated, but may also wish to create a new and distinctive route such as a relocation bulletin or news sheet.[8,10] Library staff involvement and morale at all levels are crucial to the success of the operation and good communication and publicity will help to alleviate the feeling of confusion and uncertainty which some staff experience when their normal work routines are disrupted. Good internal publicity will also encourage teamwork amongst staff from different parts of the organisation who may not be accustomed to working closely with those in other functions towards a common and immediate goal.

External publicity
An effective publicity campaign is the key to avoiding unnecessary confusion amongst users and also repetitious explanations.[15] The primary purpose is to inform the user community and other libraries about the changes taking place and, in larger moves, about the progress of the move itself. Publicity should be simple, comprehensible and positive. There are lessons from commercial companies and high street shops who tend to stress the beneficial aspects of inconvenience - 'reorganising to serve you better' and 'apologies for inconvenience - services will be better'.

The basic information to be communicated will include the dates of the move, the nature of services available during the move and contact name for any queries. It is also important to explain to readers precisely what they are required to do beforehand, for example, borrow as many books as possible or plan their inter-library loan requests in good time. Readers will expect to know and will have justifiable anxieties about access to essential information and services. Opinion varies on whether to encourage readers to borrow as many books as possible and retain them beyond the move, without the risk of fines if these apply,[16,20] - this approach means there are less books to move but provision must be made when allocating space on the shelves for the books when they are eventually returned.

Should the library remain open?

This question should be answered on the basis of local conditions, priorities and resources. The need to support the parent organisation and for public goodwill may make the additional effort essential.[6] Indeed, some libraries such as those in law firms,[22] hospitals[7] or industrial concerns[5] may not be able to close or even reduce their opening hours during a move, but for many there will be scope for redefining the opening hours and range of the service. If the library remains open then every attempt should be made to separate the users from the particular area being moved and this can be particularly difficult when moving into an extended library. It should be remembered that the move may impose unusual or even unacceptable hazards for the public. Attention will also be needed for providing the necessary staffing to maintain services.

Although some removal contractors make a point of their ability to work around readers,[16] few would challenge the assumption that a move can be achieved more efficiently and quickly with the library completely closed to readers. The removers have undisturbed access and library staff can concentrate on supervision or greater involvement as the case may be.

Many large libraries endeavour to provide some sort of temporary or emergency service. The scope of this service should be clearly defined and communicated to users well in advance and will often be a useful way of providing work for some staff during the move. The temporary service may be provided by transferring critical materials and services to a particular room or branch or, exceptionally, to temporary premises. Access to photocopiers, newspapers and the inter-library loans service are much appreciated by readers. Through a 'paging' system it may be possible to retrieve specific books and periodicals required by readers. It may also be possible to offer CD-ROM services or access to networked services from computers outside the library. The provision of a telephone help-line and a staffed information point will go a long way to alleviate the anxieties of readers during a move of more than a few days, and a flexible approach sensitive to the exceptional and urgent needs of some users during this period will gain great respect for the library.

In planning for the move, alternative arrangements for all the normal deliveries of post, books and periodicals will have to be made. Suppliers of books, periodicals and consumables should be advised as to whether deliveries should be suspended throughout the move and that arrangements for payment may be changed or suspended temporarily.

Resources

Little information is available in the literature on the cost of moves and this is not surprising in view of the range and complexity involved. As a good guide, an experienced mover should be able to pack and unload 600-700 metres a day at a cost of something like £1,000 a day in addition to which there is the cost of hiring trollies and crates and any additional office furniture and stock which may require moving. Removal contractors are experienced at costing moves and will be particularly interested in the ease of access to and egress from the buildings, the ease of movement around both sites and the size of the stock which they will often estimate for themselves based on the number of shelves.[16]

In some projects provision is made in the building grant for the cost of a move or, more likely, in the furniture grant. However 'earmarking' is a thing of the past in some sectors and resources may not be explicitly allocated for the move. The budget available may have been used up towards the end of the project when the move is considered or, even worse, the cost of the move may have been overlooked. Sometimes the library is then faced with bidding for additional resources or planning the cheapest, and not necessarily the best, move.

It is particularly difficult to accurately cost a 'do-it-yourself' move and much depends on what is included in the calculations.[8] In estimating costs a number of elements should be included.[15] For example: survey fees; van rental; temporary building modifications; trolley and crate hire; building protection; special communications (portable telephones); hoists; publicity and signing. Some damage may be sustained by books, equipment, furniture and the building, and the cost of replacement and remedial work should be estimated unless appropriate insurance has been arranged. Costs often overlooked include additional security; insurance; lost crates; and overtime or call-out costs for plant and maintenance engineers.

The building

Features of the old and new accommodation which restrict the movement of books, equipment and furniture should be identified and, wherever possible, remedial action taken. Good access to the buildings and good vertical and horizontal communication are equally important in moving libraries as they are in the planning and design of good libraries. Indeed, the ease of book movement and the layout of the loading bay will be severely tested during the relocation.

Special ramps may be required over steps and on staircases to facilitate trolley movement. The number and reliability of the lifts is often a critical constraint in the move and contractors frequently plan the flow of books so as to make optimum use of the lifts. Where the move depends upon a functioning lift a 24 hour call-out to the engineers, although expensive, will be essential. New lifts are notoriously unreliable and contingency plans must be made for the case of breakdown. In some libraries the only option is defenestration[16] and egress through the windows.[20] In fact, special insurance can be taken out against certain risks such as lift breakdown which could threaten the whole move. With new premises the move is most likely to be the first time the building services have been in operation for an extended period and reliability problems are almost inevitable.

Great care should be taken to protect the building and furniture against accidental damage. For example, doors, lifts and carpets should be covered, preferably with hardboard. Even the routes taken by trollies outside the building may be covered to facilitate smooth and easy movement.

Stock measurement and space allocation

Fundamental to library moves is the process of measuring the stock and allocating space on the shelves in the new premises. This is to ensure a quick and efficient move in which the librarian can be confident the stock will fit precisely as required and that best use has been made of the space available. Despite the profession's fondness of quoting stock sizes, in reality, few libraries know precisely how many books they have on their shelves. It is the large quantity of books and the need to preserve their sequence that sets library moves apart from others and normally represents the largest and most costly part of the move. It is also the part with the greatest potential for disaster.

The procedures developed will depend upon the library's circumstances. Some libraries where space is very limited will be interested in a precise stock measurement whilst others will be content with counting the number of shelves to be moved. Greater accuracy will be needed where collections are to be merged and sufficient space must be left for incoming collections from other sites. The sophistication of the coding system used for the new shelving arrangement will depend upon the level of precision required in the relocation. Some removal contractors[17] question the attention given by librarians to accurate stock measurement and sophisticated coding systems which, they claim, only serve to complicate the move and frustrate those unable to grasp them easily and are, therefore, counter-productive. On the other hand, a more accurate and better planned move leaves less to chance and will be quicker and smoother in the long run. It is generally better for the stock measurement and allocation to be undertaken by a professional librarian who knows the stock well. Although it is a tedious task there is no substitute for the knowledge and experience of how the collection has developed, the nature of the subject areas, current growth rates, preservation needs and patterns of use.

Stock measurement is normally recorded on standard forms designed for the purpose (see Figure 1) and these can be as simple or complex as the situation requires.[4,15,19] Space should then be allocated within the new shelving to allow for growth of the collections and distributing the stock so that particular subjects start in sensible places. Decisions will have to be made on a variety of issues such as how full the shelves are to be, whether top and bottom shelves are initially to be left vacant, and where empty bays are required for growth. The fullness of the shelves will vary throughout the collections. Shelves housing bound periodicals can be almost completely filled whereas those housing growing collections should not be filled beyond 80% of capacity.

Where a shelf-for-shelf transfer is proposed, and this is by far the simplest type of move, it may be sufficient simply to record the number of shelves in a subject area, but if greater precision is required, the number of volumes can be counted or the length of shelving occupied measured in linear metres. The height of the tallest book on each shelf, or the clearance required between it and the shelf above, is also important so that the new shelving can be adjusted to accommodate the incoming stock and optimum use made of the space available. Rather than record exact clearances the library may choose two or three standard ranges. For example, 28 cm high (sufficient for most books), 33 cm high (suitable for most quartos) and 41 cm high (books larger than this may be shelved on their side or elsewhere). Using the standard form each shelf in the old arrangement is given a code for the shelf upon which the stock will be placed in the new arrangement. Moving the books then simply becomes a matter of matching labels. An example of a sheet for recording the stock and allocating new shelves is shown in Figure 1.

11

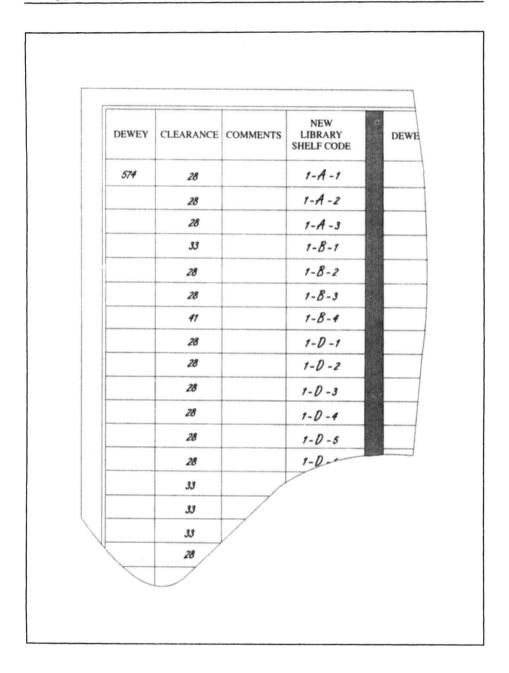

Figure 1 - Form for recording stock measurements and allocating new shelves.
Each line represents a shelf

The shelf coding system can be as sophisticated as the size and complexity of the stock and use of the library demands. A simple system of running numbers may be sufficient in a small library whilst a multi-digit system may be preferred in a large library occupying several floors. In the latter case the floors may be colour coded (e.g. blue for level 2), each range of shelving given a number, each bay a letter and each shelf in the bay a number. An example of a shelf coding system is shown in Figure 2 in which the code Blue 1B4 unambiguously specifies the fourth shelf down in bay B of range 1 on level 2. As a principle the simplest system which will facilitate a speedy and efficient move for all concerned should be used.

When filling the shelves in the new setting some libraries will choose to adjust the shelves to accommodate the incoming collections as the books are received. This requires good supervision and will delay the rate of reloading the shelves. It is generally preferable to adjust the new shelving beforehand to the heights necessary to receive the incoming books. In the example shown in Figure 1 space has been left on the bottom three shelves of bay A, the bottom shelf of bay B and all of bay C for future growth. Shelves 1B1 and 1B4 must be adjusted to provide a clearance of 33 cm and 41 cm respectively in order to accommodate the size of books to be relocated from the former premises.

When measuring the stock librarians sometimes raise the question of stock which is out on loan and express concern as to whether it can be accommodated when it is returned. Clearly, a certain proportion of the stock is always out on loan and provision need not be made for it. In a shelf-for-shelf move there should be capacity on the shelves to absorb additional stock. Where the library is very short of space and the return of books is perceived to be a problem, the automated (or manual) issue system should be capable of revealing the number of volumes on loan in particular classification categories and an appropriate allowance made when allocating the new space.

Similar principles apply to moving other stock housed on shelves - periodicals, microforms, CD-ROMS, videos etc. Children's books, unbound periodicals and government publications are reported to be less straightforward than books and bound periodicals.[16] Current periodicals, for example, are often secured together with a binding tie and treated as book 'units'.[8] Maps and photographic materials are examples of non-book media which are not normally housed on shelves but they must be assessed and given a location in the new library in much the same way, and special care is necessary in handling these items during the move.

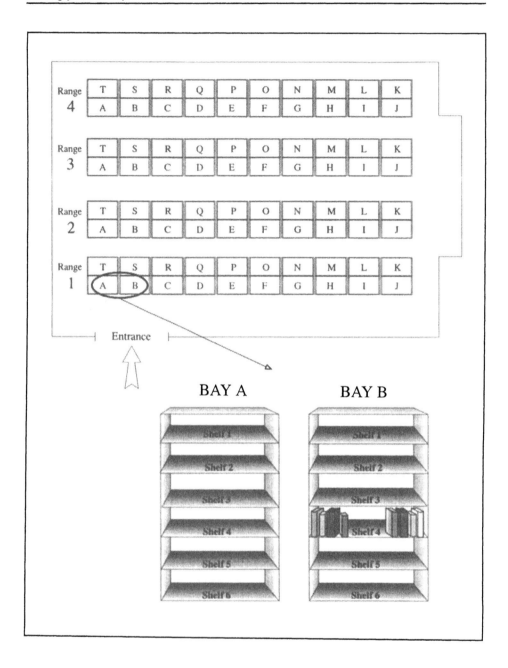

Figure 2 - Shelf coding system for the new library
In this layout the books have been placed on shelf 1B4
i.e the fourth shelf down in Bay B in Range 1

Merging collections

Providing advice upon merging collections is not easy because of the wide variety of instances involved but clearly greater attention to planning is required especially when the collections to be merged arrive at different times.[5,9] Wherever possible the integration should be planned so as to avoid secondary moves or, at most, short ones which do not require repacking.[2] Those with experience of merging collections suggest useful approaches including restricting measurement and planning to small discrete blocks of shelving (for example 40 bays or 500 metres) to localise the effects of any error, and moving the largest collection first.[8,9]

Labels

Removal contractors are normally able to supply suitable labels upon which shelf codes may be printed, often by computer. Stick-on peel-off labels should be attached to the library shelves in the old arrangement, transferred to the trollies or crates used to move that shelf of books by the packers and matched with the identical shelf codes on the shelving in the new site.[5] Where books are stored for a period of time, the labels must retain the ability to adhere.

Other techniques

Several other techniques for measuring stock are mentioned in the literature and may have applications where time is limited.[15]

Measuring the shelf list

Where an up-to-date shelf list or inventory exists on cards the size of stock can be estimated from the standard 'one inch of shelf list cards for 100 volumes'. Statistical checks can be used to verify the accuracy of the conversion factor used. The technique is most accurate in a large collection with a correspondingly large shelf list.

Automated library systems

Many automated circulation and cataloguing systems provide title and volume counts of holdings. This approach may be applicable in libraries where all the stock is recorded on the system and the file maintenance procedures are known, but is most deficient in registering periodical volumes.

Shelf capacity standards

Through sampling or using the standards given in the literature it is possible to determine the number of volumes in a particular range of shelving or in a particular area of the library.

Mathematical modelling

Formulae have been developed for collection movement and sequence distribution which even include labour estimates.[11,18]

Automated techniques
Although there seems to be no substitute for physically measuring the stock, microcomputers have been successfully used in a number of ways from simple recording and manipulation of data through to more sophisticated planning, management and control activities.[15,18] As with all automated systems the performance and potential is limited by the quality and type of information that has been fed into the system.

Simple floor-plan packages and even CAD (computer-aided design) packages have been used to assist in space allocation, and other software used to devise and print coding and numbering systems for rooms and shelves. Spreadsheet packages have been particularly effective in manipulating and presenting collection data, for reviewing several layout options and for demonstrating the consequences of different 'fill rates' and growth patterns.[8,32] The investment involved in inputting data becomes more appropriate for larger moves especially where collections will merge, and the computer can present different 'what-if scenarios' and make projections based on various 'fill rates'. This can be particularly useful when the layout of the stock has to be re-configured due to changed circumstances during the move. Lotus 1-2-3 seems to have been widely used for measurement and layout activities in the United States.[7,15,33]

Book Move Control System
The size and complexity of the transfer of collections in some libraries warrants the use of more sophisticated automated systems for the management of moves. The awesome prospect of moving 8 million volumes to one new building from sixteen different buildings when, for historical reasons, much material is out of sequence, led the British Library to develop a Book Move Control System (BMCS) to assist in the planning, monitoring and control of book relocation processes to the new building at St Pancras.[9] Basically, the system imitates the manual processes previously described. Presented with information of the available shelving in the new premises and the collections to be moved, the system will provide information for planning and implementing the moves.

The whole process has a number of phases:

> *Planning stage* - In the preliminary planning stage the storage capacity of the new shelving is estimated and a preferred arrangement of the collections determined based on shelf length. For a more detailed estimate of the collections to be moved the stock is divided into manageable sections of about 500 metres and allowances are made for growth rates and preservation space, i.e. the additional space required when material is bound or boxed. BMCS allocates space based upon details of the height, width and depth of the shelves in the new library and the length and average height of the collections. The system checks whether the collections will fit in the proposed

locations and can present alternative layouts for consideration. It also provides advance information to the library and its readers about the timing of moves, basing its predictions on the estimated length of the collections and a move rate of 400 linear metres a day.

Implementation stage - BMCS is then provided with more accurate information to ensure a precise move and one which makes optimum use of the space available in the new site. Measurements of each shelf to be moved including the height of the tallest book (see Figure 3) are recorded on portable computers and fed into the main system.

The system verifies the data checking for anomalous measurements and then produces labels for each shelf of books to be moved showing the unique shelf address in both the old and new arrangements. These are placed on shelf cards at the start of each shelf (see Figures 4 & 5). The system predicts where gaps should be left for stock to be moved and integrated in due course. It also specifies the heights to which the new shelving should be adjusted in order to accommodate the height of books to be moved.

BMCS produces labels for the crates in which the books are moved and these contain information to ensure that material is shelved in the required order (see Figure 6). It also prints control sheets for use by the supervisors. In this move the crate labels are different from the shelf labels because it is not a shelf-for-shelf move but the material will be shelved on a 'wrap round' basis in the new site. The shelf cards are included in sequence. Another unusual feature is the use of large crates in which the contents of more than one shelf are packed.

Information on the progress of the move is fed into the system on the basis of which managers and readers can be kept up to date and contractors paid. The destination information on the cards ensures the material is placed on the correct shelf and that 'creep' is controlled (Figure 7).

Clearly, the procedures and systems developed reflect the immense scale and complexity of this major national library move and also local circumstances. Although it forms an interesting case study, few libraries will need to plan for different coding systems for the old shelves and crates as well as the new shelves, and are unlikely to use the unusually large and consequently heavier crates for the book transfers. The substantial investment required to develop and implement an automated system like the Book Move Control System is only worthwhile for moves of over 5 kilometres of stock.

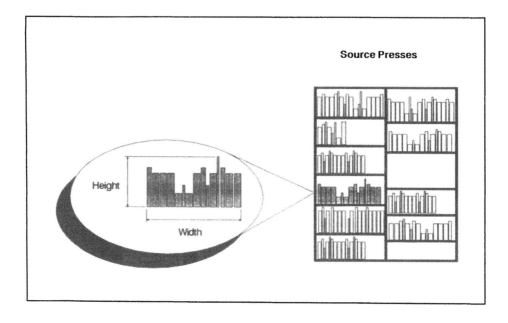

Figure 3 - Shelf measurements

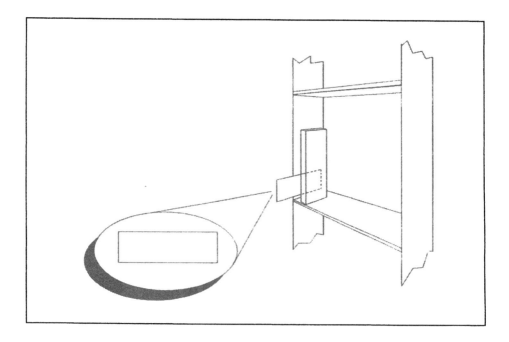

Figure 4 - Shelf cards

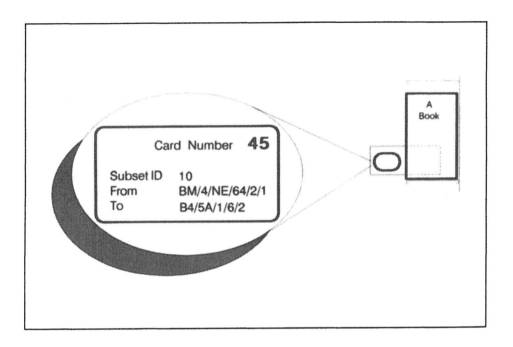

Figure 5 - Labels for shelf cards

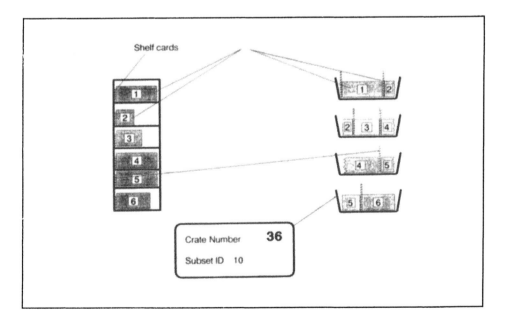

Figure 6 - Packing the crates

19

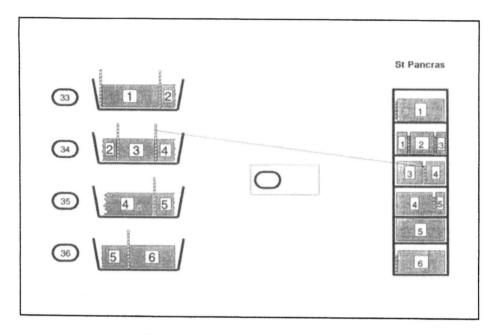

Figure 7 - Stacking at St Pancras shelves

3. The move

Method of moving

Moving a collection into a new empty space on a shelf-for-shelf basis is fairly straightforward, but if an overcrowded collection is to be re-arranged or collections merged, procedures will be more complicated. Logistics can be particularly challenging when collections are stored, when secondary moves cannot be avoided and when existing shelving must be dismantled and re-erected in the new site. There is controversy amongst those experienced in the move business as to whether trollies or crates are the better method for relocating books, and removal contractors tend to develop strong preferences. However, there is general agreement that the size of the trolley shelf or crate should be capable of accommodating one shelf of books. In reality, methods of moving appropriate to local circumstances should be used and it may be a mixture of techniques are required.

Trollies

Book trollies are popular especially when moving within a building and where lifts are provided. They are sometimes referred to as file trollies because they were originally designed for moving office files. Trollies can be easily moved across floors and into lifts and so eliminate much of the heavy lifting associated with other methods. The books can be arranged in the same sequence as on the shelf and also the same way up, minimising the risk of mixing. The trollies must be of good quality so as not to damage the books and are costly to produce. Removal contractors normally supply their own specialised trollies and these are usually constructed of wood with one solid side so that books cannot fall through. More sophisticated examples will have angled shelves to keep the books in place, carpeting for protection of the books, quick release bracing straps for security and even sheeting for weather protection to the open side.[8] Where libraries organise their own move, the substantial cost involved in constructing and maintaining trollies must be included in the estimates.

Some special libraries have chosen to use trollies as a temporary 'library' open to users. This has been found to be useful when it is impossible to close the library throughout the move.

Those not inclined towards using trollies point to the catastrophic consequences which can result when they are taken outside on uneven surfaces and are exposed to bad weather. Broken wheels and trollies which have tipped over can cause serious delays and disruption. Fully operational lifts are crucial to moves involving trollies but, even when libraries have gone to the considerable expense of 24-hour call-out maintenance, lift breakdowns will hold up trolley moves unless adequate contingency arrangements have been made. Carpets, lifts and trolley routes need protection, preferably with hardboard, and this also facilitates the easy movement of the heavy, fully laden trollies over carpets and uneven surfaces.

Crates
Many librarians and contractors prefer storage crates[9,17] and regard them as cheaper and more flexible in the long run. Crates should be sturdy, stackable and have handles for lifting. Some also have lids for protection and security. Plastic crates are most common but heavy duty cardboard[7] or fibre boxes are sometimes used and can be broken down for transport purposes.[2] Care is needed when packing and unpacking the crates to preserve the correct sequence of the books and workers sometimes need to be restrained from filling the crates with the contents of more than one shelf. Crates should be of a size capable of accommodating one shelf of books although, exceptionally, larger and consequently heavier ones have been specified.[2,9] The crates are normally stacked on trollies in reverse order to facilitate removal in the correct order at the new site.

Those with a preference for crates suggest the books are more secure and better protected, especially where lids are used. Where security is a particular concern they can be bubble-wrapped and unpacked only after security personnel have broken the seal. Crates may be the only option when the book stock has to be stored for any length of time and the cost of hiring the crates for the period in question should not be overlooked. Contractors normally hire crates and since it is not uncommon for numbers of crates to be lost or stolen during a move, attention to security and provision for replacement costs is essential.

In planning the logistics of a move special attention must be given to the pattern of movement of trollies and crates. The person coordinating the move will be eager to achieve a fast flow rate by making optimum use of the lifts, avoiding bottlenecks and by providing parking and storage areas for the trollies and crates. This is particularly important in moves where, as a result of using lorries, fork lift trucks or motorised trucks, the crates and trollies arrive in large batches.

In addition to or instead of trollies and crates, some libraries have successfully used other methods of moving[6,15] and these include:

- mechanical conveyors - these have limited value except for short distances, and cost and reliability are key concerns

- hand-passing - this may be useful for small collections over small distances and where large numbers of helpers are available

- custom-made troughs.

Whatever system is used three fundamental issues emerge:

- Expert supervision by library staff is necessary at both ends. Even with the best laid plans there is no substitute for alert well-trained supervisors at both the packing and unpacking ends to deal with the queries and difficulties which inevitably arise and which require an immediate response if delay and mistakes are to be avoided.[6] Good communication between those involved at the source and destination shelves is essential and a telephone link, two-way radio or, better still, portable telephones[14] are invaluable.

- A good shelf labelling system will clearly identify where books are to be shelved. In the new facility temporary signs, often marked-up architect's drawings, will assist workers in finding the correct location for the books. The shelf label is removed from the source shelf and fixed to the trolley shelf or crate. The label is coded for the destination shelf and simply needs to be matched with the identical shelf label in the new site to determine the correct shelf. Colour coding can be particularly helpful in providing a visible indication of which room or floor the books should be taken to.

- Good training is essential for all those involved and this includes book handling, preservation concepts, packing instructions, classification, physical safety, access arrangements and emergencies. In one library this information was distributed to all staff as a training manual.[8]

Equipment and furniture

Modern library and information services have increasing amounts of equipment and computers. The principle for relocation is just the same as for books - everything to be moved should be inspected, listed, given a location in the new premises and labelled. In general, equipment must then be decommissioned, suitably packaged, moved and recommissioned at the new site.

A good removals contractor should have the necessary experience, expertise, specialist equipment and authorisation to move most library equipment and furniture themselves. Some equipment requires special attention when moving and it is as well to contact the supplier or maintenance company for advice.[6,15] Equipment maintenance contracts often contain a clause voiding the contract if the items are moved by other than an authorised moving agent. Photocopying companies are particularly fussy in this respect and normally have a moving contract with a specialised transportation company although they may give permission for the library's remover to be used. Bindery equipment often requires specialised removers. Hoists will be needed for heavy items such as safes. Fragile equipment, for example, will need protective packing.

Computers are much less of problem than they used to be[15] but minicomputers and mainframes may have to be moved by an approved contractor after the supplier has fully decommissioned and prepared the kit.[5] Most microcomputers and peripherals can now be moved by a good moving company. Equipment is normally moved in cages and can be bubble-wrapped for additional protection and security. Highly desirable portable video and computer equipment and associated software represent a substantial security risk during moves and the librarian may wish to specify additional security measures such as a special security seal which must be broken by library or security staff before unpacking.

A useful checklist of different types of equipment and stock which might need to be considered is given in Chapter 4 of 'Creating an Information Service' by S.P. Webb.[36]

It is preferable to lock all furniture being moved and to make sure the keys are strapped to the item. A spare set of keys can be a lifesaver.[3]

Special items

Libraries have often collected valuable paintings, statues, antique furniture and other special items in addition to special collections of rare and valuable books and manuscripts. Experts on special collections and conservation and also removal contractors will give the necessary advice on moving items. The approach taken for each item will depend upon its value, rarity, condition and importance. In many cases it is a question of taking extreme care, wrapping and protecting items and giving sufficient attention to security. Bubble-wrapping and acid-free separators are often used when moving special collections. Important paintings may be wrapped to the standard sufficient for sending abroad. Additional insurance may be needed but it should be remembered that, despite their value, many items are unreplaceable and, therefore, represent an uninsurable risk.

Staff

The planning group must decide whether it is better to have the majority of staff present to assist during the move or encourage them to take leave. Many staff who remain will be unable to continue their normal work and heads of section will have the responsibility of allocating suitable work. Those participating in the move will be undertaking very different work from normal - it will be more physical, dirty and repetitive - most will rise to the occasion, others may feel less motivated. Some staff who suffer from physical conditions, such as bad backs, may be precluded from taking an active part in the move. Construction work and the movement of books often creates a considerable amount of dust and this can trigger certain occupational allergies, asthma and bronchitis.[11] Special attention will be needed to health and safety and personal security during the move.

In some cases staff are relocated early in the move to concentrate upon recommencing services from the new premises. In others they will move towards the end when the majority of stock, equipment and furniture has been transferred so that they can resume 'normal' work. Staff with responsibility for automated systems may be relocated early in the move to undertake the work necessary for recommissioning the system in the new library. Staff are often given responsibility for packing their own desk contents in crates.

Order of the move

Planning a library move involves estimating the time required for the relocation of all the various different elements of the service and putting these individual moves together in a logical, coherent and coordinated sequence so that services can recommence from the new premises as soon as is possible. Much will depend on the geography and layout of the buildings concerned and the availability of lifts, but moves often start at the top of the old premises and work downwards so that progress is increasingly less dependent on lifts and vertical communication. Clearly, the timetable must be communicated to all concerned and the planning committee should ensure that each section of the library is fully prepared for their particular part of the move. The sequence can be presented in a variety of ways and an example for a large academic library is shown in Figure 8.

Even if the bulk of the staff will not move until the end of the process it is not uncommon for a department to establish a presence in the new site at an early stage. In deciding upon an order for the relocation of the collections, librarians often prefer to transfer the largest collections first. Removals contractors are expert at devising timetables to make optimum use of the building, the staff and transport available in such a way as to avoid disruptive conflicts in the flow of work. The librarian must remain flexible and be prepared to adapt the timetable as the move develops since moves frequently proceed quicker than anticipated but, conversely, delays are not unknown when, often as a result of unforeseen circumstances, it is necessary to devise and implement alternative plans.

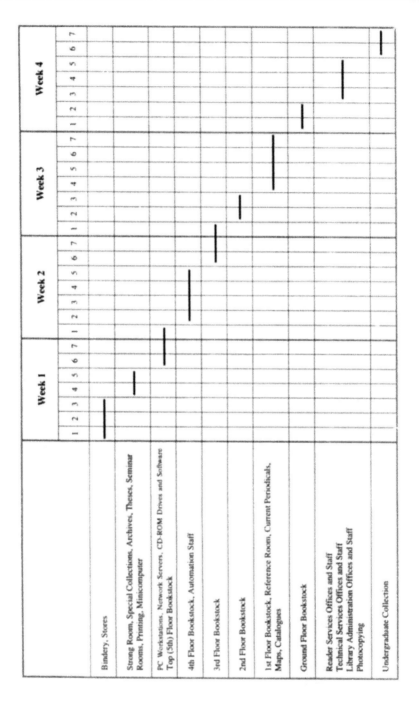

Figure 8 - Timetable for a move

Who should conduct the move?

Each library must decide the most appropriate way of moving depending upon local circumstances, resources and politics. The choice will depend upon several factors including the size and complexity of the move, the volume of stock, the distance to be moved, the budget available, the speed required and the availability of labour.

Those who may be asked to undertake the move could include:

- library staff
- temporary workers
- students
- volunteers
- professional movers.

Some small libraries with limited resources may have no option but to use their own staff for the move. Libraries often prefer to undertake the packing and unpacking themselves[8,12] even though in many cases a removals contractor can achieve and sustain a faster rate. However, the librarian may be swayed in cases where there is a need to select items for moving, where destination can only be determined upon selection, where preservation judgements are necessary and where the merging of collections makes for a complicated move. What is certain is that library personnel are essential for the close supervision of packing and unpacking and the reloading of the shelves. Even the most conscientious moving crews are understandably inclined to move as quickly as possible and this can contribute to error. A library supervisor posted at each end and in constant contact is a great remedy to potential disaster.[7]

Although using library staff may appear to be the cheapest option it should be remembered that sustained lifting and moving furniture over a period of time is physically demanding work and this can lead to stress, injuries and accidents.[6,15] The dangers and liability costs may outweigh the potential saving in labour costs. Staff contracts should be checked before asking library staff to engage in removals work. For some, enthusiasm and commitment will make it difficult to restrain their active participation: others may be less well motivated.

Temporary workers, students and volunteers are sometimes used to good effect. The librarian will be concerned to achieve a reliable and preferably unchanged workforce necessary to achieve an efficient move and work schedule. Time and resources must be spent in orientating, training and supervising these staff.[8] Each team requires good instruction regarding the sequence of the move, attention to book order and advice on the proper way of lifting to guard against injury. There are reports that staff appointed to short-term contracts can develop grievances towards the end of the project and become disruptive. There is a growing trend to offer students employment on campus but there may be certain organisational restrictions to this. Some libraries have experienced difficulty in terminating short-term workers or volunteers whose work turns out to be unsatisfactory.

In some cases libraries choose a mixture of personnel, for example using staff, students or volunteers to pack and unpack the collections and commercial movers for the transport and removal of heavy items. Where several types of assistance are used the importance of coordination, training and supervision should not be underestimated.

There is considerable disagreement and many contradictory claims over the question of costs, and comparisons can be difficult to draw since much depends upon what is included in the calculations. It has been suggested that using student labour and staff supervision can probably save as much as 50% of the cost of a professional remover.[2] Others argue differently. One library estimated the cost of completing the move itself would be three times the cost of using professionals.[14] One academic library which undertook a 'do-it-yourself' move concluded that the total cost was indeed higher than the direct charges made by some commercial movers, but noted that library staff still had to be paid whether involved in the move or not.[8] Moving a library is heavy, dirty and repetitive work and the physical stress and strain and risk of injury to staff should not be underestimated. In view of the experience and expertise contractors can contribute to the planning and execution of the move and the sustained speed they can achieve, it is likely a professional mover will provide a quicker and more cost-effective relocation in the long run.

Removal contractors
Some librarians offer persuasive arguments that professional movers can make the move more cheaply, effectively and quickly than the library staff, especially when large libraries are to be relocated some distance away. There are removal companies who specialise solely in libraries and their expertise and experience can make a significant contribution to the planning and execution of the move.[16,17] They will provide the lorries, specialised equipment, trollies, crates and labels, and their staff are trained to move items efficiently and safely.[2] They may have the necessary authority to move certain specialised items like photocopiers. Some can even assist with publicity. The mover may be employed simply to transport items or to manage the whole exercise. In employing a contractor the library is transferring the risk, releasing its staff from the physical work involved and enabling them to concentrate upon professional supervision. It should be noted that removal companies who do not have experience of moving a

library are liable to underestimate the complexity of the process,[4] e.g. companies normally involved with domestic house moves may not be the most appropriate for commercial contracts.

Because of the substantial costs involved institutional regulations normally dictate that large moves are put out to tender. Many libraries will accept the cheapest bid but there are stories of disastrous moves caused by the inadequate work of the lowest bidder.[16,17] The cheapest bid may be the costliest in the long term and may necessitate an expensive clear up. The library requires the best quality move at the lowest price and there are a number of factors which will influence the selection of the successful contractor and these include:

- previous library experience
- recommendation from librarians
- personality of those you will work with
- approach and methodology proposed
- management and supervision
- speed
- price
- performance guarantees
- professionalism
- specialised equipment, and
- insurance and security.

In analysing tenders the library should always ask for an explanation of methodology proposed, and it is worth bearing in mind that not all moving companies are independent and several may be owned by a common parent organisation. It is advisable to be as specific as possible when contracting a removals company since the lack of important details, such as the size of crates, can lead to misunderstandings and ultimately a poor job.[17] Contractual terms are likely to be established by the library's parent organisation but sample contracts are available in the literature.[15,19] Staged payment is not uncommon for large moves.

Once a contractor has been appointed it is important to plan the move together. Official lines of communication and responsibility for decision making should be established. A point of contact should be nominated at management/supervisory level in the removal company with whom the library move coordinator can liaise. Interpersonal skills will play an important part in the success of the working relationship between library and contractor.

Operational guidelines

Whoever is selected to undertake the move, the librarian should set out the principles and 'rules' involved and establish a framework for operational discipline which must be communicated to all concerned. These 'guidelines' should emphasise that:

- the sequence of library books runs from left to right, starting on the top shelf of a bay and proceeding to the shelf below when the end of the first is reached

- books should be handled carefully with their spines uppermost

- special care should be taken when handling equipment, software and non-book materials

- damage to the building and furniture should be minimised

- uncertainties and difficulties should always be checked with library supervisors -quality should not be sacrificed for speed

- the ground rules for behaviour preclude smoking, eating and drinking in the library[20] (and may refer to the playing of music)

- wherever possible, the composition of teams of workers should be unchanged.[20]

Human aspects

Much of the literature concentrates on the procedural aspects of moving libraries but, as in all areas of library management, human resources are of central importance. It is people who plan and execute moves and success depends upon their knowledge, motivation, vision, commitment, organisation and training.[2,8,14,15] The person directing the move requires good planning, communication and leadership qualities. A broad 'vision' is necessary combined with attention to detail. Good listening skills can be extremely beneficial in revealing potential problems at the coal face.[3]

Staffing and administrative problems are often greater than the physical ones.[4,12] Enhanced teamwork and commitment amongst the staff can normally be achieved through effective communication[24] and by encouraging participation.[8] Staff should feel they 'own the change'[21] and have a responsibility for achieving the success of the move. Expectations can vary dramatically from hopes for more responsibility to fears of loss of job satisfaction.[22] Staff reaction may also vary from over-enthusiasm and interference to apathy and dissatisfaction.

We shall not be moved!

It should be recognised that some staff are uncomfortable or even resistant to change, especially change of this magnitude and, whatever the qualities of the new arrangement, may feel a deep sense of commitment to the existing building. Long-standing staff have been known to display these tendencies[4] and may not wish to participate in the move and, worse still, seek to be disruptive. It may be better for these staff to be on leave during the move. Relocations involving the rationalisation of sites and consequent staff restructuring and redundancies can be plagued with bad feelings.[4,5] It is reported that one librarian lost four staff members as a result of a particularly traumatic merger and move.[23]

However, moves may also produce significant changes in established patterns of staff organisation and behaviour and have been found to have a beneficial impact on library staff attitudes and morale.[10] The move represents a common 'superordinate' goal that can only be achieved through teamwork and cooperation. Unlike some library work, achieving the move is a clear, tangible, finite and unavoidable assignment for which the consequences of failure are as attributable as they are public. During the period of the move work patterns are altered, normal rules are suspended and there is a refreshing change of pace. To prepare for this change staff may be sent on workshops away from the library, in order to bring those who are unaccustomed to working with each other together in teams, co-operating in solving problems unrelated to everyday work. After such events, staff have been found to display improved teamwork, communication, motivation, achievement and even social integration.[5,18,20,24] Some reveal hidden depths and qualities of leadership and decision-making under these unusual circumstances, and this may not necessarily reflect seniority.

The completion of a successful move will leave most staff feeling a sense of satisfaction, pride, relief, accomplishment and physical exhaustion.[10,15] Library moves are no exception to people's natural reaction to celebrate after the completion of a particularly intense task.[7,15] The staff involved in the move might very well appreciate a formal celebration of the completion of the move - at which the library manager (perhaps along with another senior executive) might be able to express gratitude and appreciation for effort and the contribution made by everyone concerned.

Security, safety and insurance

Moving a library creates particular security risks[6] arising from operating on both old and new sites for a limited period with stock, equipment and furniture moving between them. During the move it becomes difficult to observe normal security routines and library materials may be particularly at risk from loss, theft or damage. It is reported that highly desirable portable video and computer equipment and software may be particularly at risk. Vulnerable equipment and also special collections are often moved in sealed boxes and only unpacked once the security seal has been broken by authorised personnel. Some librarians suggest going even further and recommend spot checks of coats and parcels and random investigation of boxes and trollies.[15] The crates themselves used in the move are liable to theft. Library staff, temporary helpers and volunteers may not be used to heavy repetitive work, physical work and may be susceptible to strain and injury. Additional staff will be working in the library who are not so familiar with the library's safety and security policy requirements. Neither the library's nor the organisation's health and safety staff will have had experience of the new building, and fire evacuation procedures are unlikely to have been resolved.

It is essential to recognise the security risks to the buildings, the collections and the people involved at an early stage and make sure the library is adequately insured. A commercial moving company may offer suitable insurance but if the library is arranging the move itself then the librarian should consult with the parent company and its insurers. The whole move can be delayed by unsuspected events, including lift breakdowns and bad weather, and insurance can be taken out against some of these risks.

Sources of advice

It is essential to seek such advice at an early stage in the planning process to avoid any potential difficulties, but the above specialists can also be called in as required, should unexpected problems arise. What may seem like an insurmountable hurdle could be a regular occurrence for the expert.

Apart from consulting the relatively modest published literature on the subject, librarians can seek advice on moves from a variety of sources:

- in-house office management services (who may also have useful contacts)
- professional library and information associations
- specialist library and information consultants
- commercial removers
- facilities management specialists
- management consultants with experience in this field
- other librarians with recent experience.

4. Conclusion

"Expect the unexpected and plan for it"[8]

Despite the best laid plans things can go wrong and often as a result of unforeseen circumstances - lift breakdowns, extremes of weather, road repairs, late deliveries, ventilation system breakdowns and strikes have all been known to disrupt library moves.[5,14,20,24] Severe delays have resulted from uncompleted building work, unfinished access routes, loss of labels, security problems, mislaid keys and shelving layouts which differ from architect's drawings upon which planning was based. The library manager must measure, plan, involve all personnel and bear in mind that no matter how much advance preparation takes place, mistakes and crises are an inevitable part of the process - at best the librarian can ensure that potential problems are minimised.[7] Recently, in some libraries, the planning period necessary to prepare adequately for the move has been reduced to as little as a few weeks, and yet the pressure to control costs and demonstrate value for money remains.

Moves can be exhausting, stressful, frustrating, dirty, time-consuming and utterly defeating.[25] Tempers may shorten. The mental and physical strain can be intense[14] and the move demands constant and accurate supervision in a high-pressure environment constrained by the budget and time.[11] On the other hand, a well-executed move can be an extremely satisfying managerial achievement[2,14] and will do a great deal of good for the library. Users and members of the parent organisation will be impressed and the reputation of the library and the confidence in its abilities will be enhanced. The profile[22] and visibility of the library will be increased and the awareness of its collections and services heightened. The librarian should build on the positive staff attributes which emerged during the move and should continue the 'planning culture'.

Some users and staff may have unrealistic expectations that everything will be better in the new library - missing books will reappear and the number of staff and computers will be increased.[25] In management terms the move can be viewed as merely a means to an end and, following a period of adjustment in the new premises, the library can concentrate on providing the improved quality of services to users the new library was planned to deliver. Nevertheless it is to be hoped that at the official opening, when tributes are paid perhaps to the skill of the architect, the patience of the users and the industry of the contractors, that a word of praise is given to the librarian and the library staff involved for the *considerable* achievement of a successful move.[26]

References

1   Parkinson, J. An Unsettling Experience: or Four Laboratories in Search of a Single Site. *Aslib Proceedings,* April 1991, 43(4), pp 137-142

2   Metcalf, K.D. *Planning Academic and Research Library Buildings, 2nd edition* by P.D. Leighton and D.C. Weber. Chicago & London: American Library Association, 1986

3   Grey, B.J. Making your Move. *American Libraries,* April 1992, pp330-331.

4   Grimwood-Jones, D. A Quick Guide to Moving Libraries. *Aslib Information,* January 1993, 21(1) p17

5   Lumley, A., Datta, V.K. & Wright, J.A. Merging and Moving - the NRI Experience: An Exercise in Library Integration and Relocation. *Aslib Proceedings,* 1991, 43(4), pp115-132

6   Holt, R.M. *Planning Library Buildings and Facilities: From Concept to Completion.* Metuchen & London: Scarecrow, 1989. (Scarecrow Library Administration Series No. 9)

7   Roth, B.R. Moving a Medical Center Library. *Special Libraries,* Winter 1985, 76(1), pp31-34

8   Bayne, P.S. The "Do-it-Yourself" Move for a 1.5 Million-Volume Library. *College and Research Libraries,* 1990, 51(1), pp55-67

9   Greenwood, D. & Shawyer, J. Moving the British Library - the Book Control System. *Aslib Information,* January 1993, 21(1), pp28-31

10   Moreland, V.F., Robison, C.L. & Stephens, J.M. Moving a Library Collection: Impact on Staff Morale. *The Journal of Academic Librarianship,* 1993, 19(1), pp8-11

11   Kurkul, D.L. The Planning, Implementation, and Movement of an Academic Library Collection. *College and Research Libraries,* July 1983, 44(4), pp220-234

12   Will, L. Imperial College and Science Museum Libraries: Working Together. *Aslib Information,* January 1993, 21(1), pp26-27

13   Seaman, S. & DeGeorge, D. Selecting and Moving Books to a Remote Depository: A Case Study. *Collection Management,* 1992, 16(1), pp137-142

14   Chepesiuk, R. An Anatomy of a Move: The Clemson University Library Special Collections. *Wilson Library Bulletin,* June 1991, 65(10), pp32-35, 155

15   Fraley, R.A. & Anderson, C.L. Library Space Planning: *A How-To-Do-It Manual for Assessing, Allocating and Reorganizing Collections, Resources and Facilities.* New York & London: Neal-Schuman, 1990. (How-To-Do-It Manuals For Libraries, Number 5)

16   Myers, C. A Mover that only Moves Libraries. *American Libraries,* April 1992, pp332-333

17   Tanner, S. Help the Removal Company to Help You. *Aslib Information,* January 1993, 21(1), p18

18   Cravey, P.J. & Cravey, G.R. The Use of Computer Modeling to Redistribute a Library's Collection. *Technical Services Quarterly,* 1991, 8(3), pp25-33

19   Kurth, H.K. and Grim, R.W. *Moving a Library.* New York & London: Scarecrow Press, 1966

20   Goodliffe, T. Waterloo to Vauxhall: Leaving County Hall. *Aslib Information,* January 1993, 21(1), pp19-21

21   Curzon, S.C. *Managing Change.* New York & London: Neal Schuman, 1989 (How To-Do-It Manuals for Libraries, Number 2)

22   Rochford, H. From Basement Blues to the Upwardly Mobile Library: Planning a Move. *The Law Librarian,* March 1992, 23(1), pp2-6

23   Hamilton, C.J. Movers, Mergers and Mayhem. *Aslib Proceedings,* 1991, 43(4), pp109-114

24   Laffoon, C.J., Richardson, G.T. & Melhorn, W.N. Relocating a Science Library: How to Cope with Plans Gone Awry! *Science & Technology Libraries,* 1991, 12(1), pp91-97

25   Duncan, M. Editorial. *Aslib Information,* January 1993, 21(1), p3

26   Thompson, G. *Planning & Design of Library Buildings.* 3rd ed. London: Butterworth, 1989

27   Schuyler, J.A. Moving Library Procedure *in* Mount, E. *Planning the Special Library.* New York: Special Libraries Association, 1972

28   Moran, R.F. Moving a Large Library. *Special Libraries,* April 1972, 63(4), pp163-171

29   Lumb, A.E. Moving an Academic Library: A Case Study. *Journal of Librarianship,* October 1972, 4(4), pp253-271

30   Brogan, L.L. & Lipscomb, C.E. Moving the Collections of an American Health Sciences Library. *Bulletin of the Medical Library Association,* October 1982, 70(4),

pp374-379

31   Spyers-Duran, P. *Moving Library Materials*. Milwaukee: Library Association of University of Wisconsin-Milwaukee, 1964

32   Ault, L.W.S. *Electronic Spreadsheets for Libraries*. Phoenix: Oryx Press, 1986

33   Carlson, B.A. Using Lotus 1-2-3 to Shift and Maintain a Serials Collection. *The Serials Librarian,* December 1987, 13, p43

34   Compton Ellis, J. Planning and Executing a Major Bookshift/Move Using an Electronic Spreadsheet. *College and Research Libraries* News, May 1988, p283

35   Mount, E. editor. *Creative Planning of Special Library Facilities*. New York: Haworth Press, 1988.

36   Webb, S.P. *Creating an Information Service,* 2nd edition. London: Aslib, 1988

www.ingramcontent.com/pod-product-compliance
Ingram Content Group UK Ltd.
Pitfield, Milton Keynes, MK11 3LW, UK
UKHW020347010325

455677UK00021B/331